BRITAIN IN OLD PHOTOGRAPHS

AROUND KNOWLE & DORRIDGE

C H A R L E S   L I N E S

ALAN SUTTON PUBLISHING LIMITED

Alan Sutton Publishing Limited
Phoenix Mill · Far Thrupp · Stroud
Gloucestershire · GL5 2BU

First published 1996

Cover photographs: *front:* a view of the White Swan and shops from between the wars; *back:* A First World War family group at Chessetts Wood.

British Library Cataloguing in Publication Data.
A catalogue record for this book is available from the British Library.

ISBN 0-7509-0817-3

Typeset in 9/10 Sabon.
Typesetting and origination by
Alan Sutton Publishing Limited.
Printed in Great Britain by
Ebenezer Baylis, Worcester.

The Revd Z.A. Antile, visiting priest from Nigeria, and the Revd J. Staples (curate) survey the village from the church tower, 1971. It is interesting to compare this view with that of 1914. Milverton Villas are prominent.

Contents

ASSOCIATION

For the DEFENCE of

The Town and Parifh of SOLIHULL,

The Town and Hamlet of KNOWLE, and the Parifh of ELMDON, in the County of Warwick.

At a Meeting held the 27th of April, 1798, at the TOWN HALL, in SOLIHULL, IT WAS UNANIMOUSLY RESOLVED,

THAT it be reprefented to the LORD LIEUTENANT, that We, the under-figned, will affociate together, and form

A TROOP OF HORSE,
TO CONSIST OF FIFTY, OR UPWARDS.

THAT we will take the Oath of Allegiance, and defend to the utmoft of our Power our moft GRACIOUS KING and our HAPPY CONSTITUTION.

THAT as our Troop will confift chiefly of Tradefmen and Farmers, who have Families, it will be a material Injury to our Trades and Bufineffes, and great Diftrefs to our Families, to be fent a great Diftance from our Home---We therefore offer our Services to aid the Civil Magiftrate more effectually to defend Property and fupprefs Riot and Tumult within the Town and Parifh of SOLIHULL, the Town and Hamlet of KNOWLE, and the Parifh of ELMDON, comprizing a Diftrict of confiderable Extent, without any Expence to Government; yet we are not willing to be liable to be ordered on Service beyond the Limits of fuch Parifhes or Hamlet, but with our Confent.

THAT JOSEPH HARDING, Efq; is nominated our CAPTAIN, and THOMAS CHATTOCK, Gent. our LIEUTENANT; and that the Lord Lieutenant be requefted to recommend thofe Gentlemen to be approved and appointed by Government.

THAT each of us will ferve without Pay, and will at his own Expence provide himfelf with a Horfe, Uniform, Arms, and Accoutrements, and that we will be trained and difciplined.

THAT the Uniform fhall be a blue Frock, red Cape and Cuffs, red Waiftcoat, Leather Breeches, round Hat and Feather, yellow Buttons, with the Letters S. K. & E. A.

THAT upon our Honour we will attend the above named Officers, or either of them, when required, for the feveral Purpofes herein ftated.

THAT we will elect a Committee, to confift of nine, of whom three fhall be competent to tranfact the Bufinefs of this Society.

THAT the Committee fhall fet on foot a Subfcription for raifing a Fund adequate to the Expence of this Undertaking, and whatever Fund fhall be fo raifed, fhall be at the fole Difpofal of fuch Committee, and they fhall appoint a Treafurer.

Jofeph Harding	Philip Holmes	James Bate
Thomas Chattock	Charles Curtis	William Tabberner
Judd Harding	Thomas Smith	John Palmer
Jofeph Wefton	Thomas Swadkins	A. Boot
James Green	William Chefhire	Jofeph Capner
Jofeph Cooke	Stephen Sprigg	Thomas Baldwin
Thomas Thompfon	William Gopfill	John Baldwin, Jun.
John Clarke	William Tomlinfon, Jun.	Jofeph Chambers
William Dawes	Jofeph Capner	Richard Chattock
Thomas Compton	John Slater	Richard Tabberner
Thomas Adrian, Jun.	William Wilfon	Jofeph Lindopp
Jofeph Clarke, Jun.	William Lewin	George Banefter.
Thomas Marfhall	William Gibbs	

A poster for the local Home Guard in time of danger from France, 1798. Thomas Marshall, innkeeper and Joseph Lindopp were Knowle men. Was William Wilson the Revd William Wilson – father of William Henry Bowen Jordan Wilson, the rakish squire who had to sell the Knowle Hall estate and emigrate to America? The troop must have cut quite a dash in those uniforms!

Introduction

When I was very young, Father bought his first motor car. My sire's driving skills would scarcely suit today's roads, but I am eternally grateful to him for an introduction to the region I seek to cover in this book. This was the Knowle where, for instance, the Greswolde Arms then boasted 'Good Accommodation for Hunters' in very big letters. Dorridge was then a small place with no bewildering road complex linking quite different villages together. There were also such delights as Umberslade's deer park (alas, no deer now) and Packwood House, where Father recalled high wooden gates that opened and closed when driving through the charming outer courtyard. We found the secluded church at Baddesley Clinton, visited Hampton-in-Arden and Barston which in that far off epoch drew no protest about airport noise; in fact, nobody dreamed of any airport at all.

Rather older, I would take the bus from Solihull to pore over 'The Records of Knowle', a precious volume incredibly left for all to peruse in the ancient Guild House. Near to hand, I would be amused by such notices as 'The church thief had been in the neighbourhood lately; he wouldn't have got much out of this box!' I found Temple Balsall, where time stood still, and explored deserted railway lines. Years later, there was tea with kindly Thomas Ferrers in Baddesley's Great Hall, dinner with the 'Felons' at Knowle's Red Lion, and at the Arden Club in Dorridge; the latter's traditional menu including tripe and saddle of lamb. So many new friends were made. Old stories also emerged; it is better just to hint about a schoolmaster who suddenly vanished, never to be seen again in his locality. Elsewhere, there was the 'Squire' and vicar who did not see eye to eye, incidentally they did not take tea together; and the scion of a certain family despatched, one surmised, to New Zealand as a 'black sheep'.

The result? Neither a guidebook nor detailed history, rather a somewhat convoluted journey, a sort of 'tapestry' of an ever-threatened, but still beloved Arden. Even with its many demolitions and changes, it is still an area of fascination. Doubtless more pictures and stories will come to light; corrections too, but the task has been rewarding.

This picture is not, as first suggested, the annual meeting of the Knowle Association for the Prosecution of Offenders, usually called the 'Felons'. It is possibly a dinner in honour of General Sir Walter Ludlow, on the occasion of his knighthood, and is held in the George Hotel, Solihull. He had close associations with Knowle and Dorridge. Several well-known Knowle residents can be identified on the photograph; H.C. Smith on the right, seems to be the Chairman whilst the second row of three are Sgt. Major Lee, Arthur Everton and Charles Wilcox (grandson of Mrs King of the post office.) C.R.M. Parr could be facing Wilcox.

The Knowle Association, established in 1800, was one of many formed in the country by landowners, farmers and others, when there was great discontent and distress among working folk owing to the high price of wheat. This was due to the operation of the Corn Laws coupled with bad harvests. This resulted in rioting, arson, maiming of cattle and theft, with gangs from Birmingham joining in.

Incidentally, the annual meeting of the 'Felons'–chiefly a social event today, is always held in November, so there would not be tulips on the table as seen in this picture!

KNOWLE

Early motorists – goggles, veils, thick coats – driving through Knowle may have thought it a sleepy sort of place. A place where nothing much had ever happened or disturbed quietude save the sound of blacksmith's hammer or church bells. They would have been mistaken, little knowing that, once, a Royal stud of sixty horses was here, and that its owner, King Edward I, gave the manor of Knowle to the monks of Westminster in his beloved wife's memory – a manor that in course of time would pass to Elizabeth I's Robert Dudley, Earl of Leicester, and to the Grevilles of Warwick Castle, one the great Sir Fulke Greville, Baron Brooke, poet and statesman and Treasurer of the Navy, another 'Fanatic Brooke', who perished with a Civil War bullet fired from Lichfield Cathedral.

Unless keen historians, they probably would not know that a wealthy cleric and diplomat, one Walter Cook, Canon of Lincoln and of Knowle stock, built the exceptionally beautiful church dedicated with ceremony in 1402. Or that, with others, he founded a guild and a college of priests, the former with its masses and social life drawing members bearing grand names or humble, from near and far. Would they know that when the shimmer of candles in chantries had been forgotten, Ephraim Huitt, 'Preacher' at Knowle and Wroxall, who fell out with Archbishop Laud, went with Warwickshire Greswolds – or should we say Griswolds? – for a new life across the Atlantic?

Would they know of Cromwellian troops clattering through, or quartered here, or John Wesley preaching in the Red Lion yard and stigmatizing Knowle as ungodly and drunken? Unfair, one thinks, as the people had valiantly saved their church after the Dissolution. Perhaps catching sight of the various inns, the intrepid motorists might think of daily coaches raising the dust, bringing gossip and news of Waterloo, travellers weary with a far from romantic journey; dangerous too through fear of 'gentlemen of the road'! (Knowle, like anywhere else had experience of highwayman and footpad, as it did of the Birmingham mob – 'Close your shutters, lock your doors!' – when it came noisily though eager to witness a public hanging in Warwick.) Someone might tell them that a great literary figure, Walter Savage Landor, received schooling in Knowle, that visitors had included the great John Constable, as well as Lady Byron, the poet's widow, who was a local landowner, as was a certain rakish, but somehow lovable, squire who was to lose his fine estate and emigrate to America.

As now, there would be the good smell of new bread, if no longer of malt: in 1830 one malster is also listed as a corkscrew-maker, together with John Kimbell, surgeon, young ladies' schools, farmers and victuallers, an *aqua-fortis* manufacturer, and Widow Smith, wheelwright.

Upright in their 'motors' giving a splendid view of the Warwickshire countryside, so often denied to their descendants in low-slung cars, the sightseers, a little fearful of breakdowns in King Edward's golden days would not dream of a trophy of a German gun (not there today) outside church and Guild House, billeted American servicemen en route for Normandy, traffic and more traffic, and all the new roads and homes to come; though they may well have considered moving out from Acocks Green; this was, in fact, becoming 'the thing'. And nobody pictured French or oriental restaurants – or that long-promised bypass!

A view from Knowle church tower, apparently showing imminent departure for Warwick Races, before 1902. In the background is the Red Lion, long before restoration. Midland Red buses to Birmingham had their terminus here with service starting just prior to the First World War.

Knowle Church tower, 1914, with open ground and gardens to the left – no thought then of the village hall, St John's Close or the shopping precinct! Knowle Lodge and the High Street with a solitary vehicle are prominent, together with the old Midland Bank building. Solihull Church steeple is just visible on the horizon.

'This fine old collegiate church strikes the eye on entering the village, as far beyond the requirements of the parish', says a nineteenth-century writer. He and the Victorian lady in the low carriage would be astounded by today's large and enthusiastic congregations.

Knowle Parish Church and – prior to restoration – the Guild House, which has had various owners and uses; it was once the post office. Only parochial from 1850, the church is owed to Canon Walter Cook, Knowle's medieval benefactor. Pinnacled external grandeur is a prelude to a splendid screen, misericords, fine windows and the Soldiers' Chapel.

Canon Thomas William Downing, beloved, outspoken Vicar of Knowle (1901–32). The photograph is particularly poignant; it was found in the pocket of Downing's ward, Harvey Watts, pierced by the shrapnel that killed him in the First World War. The Canon helped passing vagrants with cash, railway tickets and clothing. They always promised to repay, 'when times were better'. These never seemed to arrive.

The Revd James William Sharp succeeded Canon Downing as Vicar of Knowle in 1933. Previously curate of Dorridge, he held the living until 1961. 'Between them', says Eva Wootton, 'he and Canon Downing were vicars for over sixty years and in some intangible way kept alive the spirit of village life'.

Samuel Davy on his ninetieth birthday. Born in 1864, he came with his father from Cumberland, took his first farm on the Brownsover estate, near Rugby and studied agriculture and land agency, removing to Knowle in 1893. He founded the firm of Samuel Davy and Son, served as parish councillor, rural district councillor, school manager, parish overseer and trustee of Knowle United Charities, and was a leading judge of cattle and sheep. He died in 1956.

Alderman James Davy, Samuel's son born 1896, second Mayor of Solihull. He and his brother Alfred died within a few weeks of each other in 1970.

The Davy brothers, Peter (right) and Richard, grandsons of Samuel Davy, and third generation to run the family business at Milverton House. This has now been taken over by another firm.

Alfred Davy, Samuel's son born 1894, with a fellow guest at a family wedding. After serving with the Warwickshire Yeomanry in the First World War, he later had 'the unique and macabre experience of seeing his own headstone in the war cemetery in the Dardanelles, Gallipoli', says Eva Wootton. He had been shot through the head. The War Office insisted he was dead, although he had been sent back to England, and his parents informed that he was alive.

Ladders proclaim additional uncovering of timbers at Milverton House, *c.* 1970. This is said to be on the site of Walter Cook's reputed birthplace. It was long the Davy family offices, as it is of their successors. In 1913, Louisa Harding had £1 per annum, payable at Christmas, and 'a good load of manure for the garden', for lighting a fire each morning, dusting and other necessaries.

Milverton Villas, a good example of Neo-Jacobean architecture (*c.* 1840), reminding us of Mrs Gaskell's day: genteel gossip, indoor caps, muffins and the tinkle of teaspoons by the fire on winter afternoons.

Knowle has long been famous for its butchers. This shop (now Sodens) is still in existence, as are others not far away. Earlier owners were Mullard and Whitehead. There is no Mullard here now, but the shop is still in business.

The fifteenth-century White Swan, the Red Lion's erstwhile neighbour, would have welcomed members of the Knowle Guild, and once boasted a bowling green as well as a quoits club; little is known of the latter, but a trophy exists. Four-poster beds, mahogany and Windsor chairs and 'about 18 spittoons' figured in a sale of 1879.

The Square, Knowle, before the First World War. The Red Lion to the left was described in 1900 as 'a family and commercial inn and posting house (George Blakemore, prop.), horses and carriages of every description on hire, every accommodation for pic-nic parties and cyclists at moderate charges'. Knowle's last surviving bowling green is now lost.

A view from between the wars, with the White Swan (now demolished), and shops still in busy occupation today, though names inevitably have changed.

A meet of hounds outside the newly restored Guild House – perhaps the last at this spot. The photograph was sent as a Christmas card in 1913. American servicemen used the Guild House for recreation in the Second World War. Some eighty Coventry folk slept there nightly in the Blitz, others elsewhere in Knowle.

The Berrow Cottage Homes (centre) supplanted a village green on which stood the stocks, and was rented by the landlord of the Mermaid for a bowling club. In 1792 it was patronised by gentry and clergy.

The death of the White Swan. Advertised for sale before the Second World War, it was replaced by shops, a swan symbol on the new buildings. Some of its timbers are incorporated in a house in Baker's Lane, not far away; others are reputedly in store. The sign bracket was transferred to the Red Lion.

High Street, looking towards Chester House and the Greswolde Arms about the turn of the century. The cottages have been replaced by shops, but despite many changes the street still has character.

A cottage beside the present Kimbell's Walk, before conversion. It was known as Kingscote when used as Knowle post office, after this was removed from the Guild House.

Kingscote after conversion, but still retaining something of its old character, even if Cotswold stone is perhaps a little incongruous. The present post office is nearby, with a large depot south of the street.

Chester House, High Street, once a farmhouse, is a fine example of fifteenth- or sixteenth-century timber-framing, and is shown here when it was Pickering's antique shop. The Knowle Society played a conspicuous part in urging the local authority to preserve the house, now a branch library.

The sad rear of Chester House before restoration. Solihull Metropolitan Borough Council has made a delightful 'knot' garden with viewing platform between the house and a service-road.

A greatly respected resident, and familiar figure in the High Street and elsewhere in Knowle, Eva Wootton, writer and artist, did sterling work for village and people with *The History of Knowle*, published for the Knowle Society in 1972. Without her diligent labours much of local life and history would never have been recorded. She died in 1981.

Another High Street figure, Charles T. Clarke (died 1931) was manager of the Knowle branch of the Midland Bank. Churchwarden and treasurer of the Men's Institute, he is described by Eva Wootton as 'a man of great rectitude and one who inspired confidence'. Mr Clarke was a very important man in the community when the Midland was the only bank in Knowle.

An early picture of Curtis's Traditional Bakery, which was established in about 1906.

A carnival scene, photographed by Peter Pickering of Chester House.

Enlarged in Georgian times, once a noted coaching inn and haunt of hunting-men, the Greswolde Arms takes its present name from Henry Greswold(e) Lewis, joint lord of the manor. It was originally the Mermaid, but was later known as Mermaid and Greswolde, or the Greswolde Arms. Lady Byron, the poet's widow, stayed here in 1843. There are many spellings of the name Greswolde. Henry Greswold(e) Lewis, joint lord of the manor of Knowle, added a final 'e' to the more usual version. Descendants of those who crossed the Atlantic are usually 'Griswolds'.

The Greswolde Arms in a later picture. No one dreamed of American servicemen in Knowle. They liked the inn, if not 'Time please' and 'please drain your glasses'! The Red Lion was also much frequented, and there was a warm welcome at the Men's Institute.

The erection of a 16 ft maypole, decked with flowers and greenery, was an important Knowle event, children dancing around it, and afterwards receiving sweets, tea and an orange, and running races. Master of Ceremonies, Mr A.H. Peach, stands in the middle of the High Street in this photograph dated 1910.

A gathering of the local Friendly Societies, Oddfellows and (presumably) Foresters – although the original caption is unclear – with banners and insignia at Knowle Lodge, the Bowers' home, during an annual procession around the neighbourhood, 1895. Much festivity would follow, with ox- and pig-roasting and a fair. Knowle Lodge has now been demolished.

The Wilson Arms, once the Rising Sun, takes its name from the first Wilson family of Knowle Hall, the Georgian frontage contrasting with timber work dating from about 1600. A former garage to the left is now linked to the main building. Mass was said in the assembly room after the destruction of the Roman Catholic church in Station Road in 1934.

This venue is apparently the Wilson Arms, but the occasion is not known.

Cricketers on the Hampton Lane (now Hampton Road) ground. The picture is undated but appears to be about 1910.

A group at a football match in what is now Hampton Road, *c.* 1920.

One of the most beautiful timber-framed homes in the Midlands, Grimshaw Hall dates from Elizabethan times, or slightly later, and for years belonged to the prominent Grimshaw family. Subsequently occupied by farmers, it was partly restored in 1886, but trees and creeper still encroached and little seems to have been done to the interior.

Grimshaw Hall, 1933. Despite earlier restoration work, when the house was bought by Mr and Mrs Murray in 1913, they found potatoes stored in the drawing-room, panelling painted and holes in the roof! Much work was carried out for them by Birmingham architect W.A. Harvey. The house was visited by Queen Mary in 1927.

The Home Guard on parade, apparently off Hampton Road.

VJ Day celebrations in Hampton Road.

The one-time ford on the River Blythe looks innocent enough here, but severe flooding in winter effectively prevented access to the mother-church at Hampton-in-Arden. It was imperative, therefore, that Knowle's chapel should remain after the Dissolution. Thanks to Knowle folk, it did.

The last delivery, 1971. Arthur Burton with Jorrocks, when the dairy business was closed.

A Standard IV school group with Miss Bates, 1908. The school was in Kenilworth Road. Miss C.M. Adderley, one of identical twins (see below), tells that by the 1950s it was terribly overcrowded, but had excellent examination results.

A school group, with the Adderley twins in the centre, 1950s.

Kenilworth Road, Knowle.   6.

In Kenilworth Road, with its variety of architectural styles and modern offshoots, the Victorian school has been converted attractively into the Royal British Legion homes, and a one-time village stores has become a French restaurant. Walter Savage Landor attended a boarding school at the Manor House (not shown), run by Thomas Treherne junior. The former police station is on the right.

The lock-keeper and his family at Knowle Locks, Kenilworth Road, 1978. The canal reached Knowle at the end of the eighteenth century. In 1802 Henry Fitchard was drowned in the 'Navigation', his funeral costing £1 2s. The locks were widened, and reduced from six to five, to allow for 100 ft boats, but they never used the canal.

The well-known Sunny Mount in Kenilworth Road, a delightful and substantial house built at about the beginning of the present century, and typical of its time. Long the home of Mr and Mrs H.C. Smith, it was sold in 1950 following Mrs Smith's death and is now a home for people with learning disabilities.

Harry Charles Smith, invariably spoken of as 'H.C. Smith', was elected first chairman of the new Solihull Urban District Council, for the years April 1932 to April 1933, but died in December 1932. He was people's warden for Knowle parish church, school manager and trustee of Knowle United Charities. Peter Davy writes: 'My grandfather H.C. Smith was also a member of Birmingham City Council, and Warwickshire County Council. He was also a magistrate. He also farmed 800 acres at Hampton Lucy and was Chairman of H.C. Smith Ltd., wholesale warehousemen, in Birmingham, Manchester and Sheffield. Eva Wootton commented: 'The years 1931 and 1932 were sad ones for the village, for no fewer than six of its best known, kindest, and most helpful men died during this time.' They also included Major Everitt, the 'Squire', and Canon Downing.

To the Memory of
BENJAMIN PALMER Esq. of OLTON
who Died the 13. of June 1772
In the 61. Year of His Age.
"He walked with God and He was not ;
For God took Him" Genesis.

Perhaps Benjamin Palmer's epitaph at Solihull is a trifle tactless. Hutton, the Birmingham historian, describes him thus: 'although six feet five inches in height, his legs were so short that he only had the walk of a small child'. A Greswold descendant, he bought the manor of Knowle in 1754, and through him it descended to the Wilsons.

Known as 'Gumley' Wilson from a Leicestershire estate he leased, William Henry Bowen Jordan Wilson succeeded to Knowle. Handsome, charming, generous, plausible and a great sportsman, he ruined himself through (metaphorically) 'always wanting green peas at Christmas' (the title of his reminiscences). He emigrated to America, aided by old servants who loved him, eventually returning for good and dying in penury.

'Gumley' Wilson pulled down most of this Knowle Hall, leaving just a shooting-box and intending to build a new mansion. Apparently of sixteenth-century origin, it was much enlarged by Fulke Greville, later fifth Baron Brooke of Warwick Castle, after his marriage in 1664 to Sarah Dashwood, daughter of a wealthy London alderman and merchant. It was noted for magnificent panelling and ceilings. In 1994 a stucco fragment of the Greville crest was found during a 'dig' carried out by the Solihull Archaeological Group, finds also including coins and pottery.

THE KNOWLE HALL ESTATE,

WARWICKSHIRE,

WITHIN ABOUT TEN MILES OF BIRMINGHAM.

A VERY IMPORTANT

FREEHOLD AND PART COPYHOLD ESTATE,

COMPRISING

KNOWLE HALL,

SIXTEEN HUNDRED AND SIXTY ACRES OF LAND,

ABOUT FORTY HOUSES AND COTTAGES,

IN AND SURROUNDING THE TOWN OF KNOWLE,

THE PERPETUAL CURACY AND THE MANOR OF KNOWLE,

Altogether producing a Rental of upwards of

£3,200 PER ANNUM,

WILL, ON THE TWELFTH DAY OF JUNE, 1849,

And next following Day, at Eleven o'Clock in the Morning, for Twelve precisely, be

OFFERED BY PUBLIC AUCTION,

AT THE HOUSE OF

MR. MARSHALL, THE GRESWOLDE ARMS INN, AT KNOWLE,

BY E. AND C. ROBINS AND CO.,

In the following Lots, subject to Conditions then and there to be produced—comprising

FARMS, FARM HOUSES, FARM BUILDINGS,

ACCOMMODATION LANDS,

TRADESMEN'S HOUSES, PRIVATE RESIDENCES, & COTTAGES & GARDENS,

In and near Knowle, and in the Parishes of Solihull and Hampton-in-Arden,
in the County of Warwick.

PRINTED BY J. W. SHOWELL, 26, TEMPLE-STREET, BIRMINGHAM.

The melancholy sale of the Knowle Hall estate, and what remained of the old mansion, took place on 12 June 1849. The Lordship of the manor actually remained with 'Gumley' for a time; after two sales it was reunited with the estate by Major S.G. Everitt.

The present Knowle Hall from the park lake. Originally three-storeyed, it was built in classical style for Robert Emilius Wilson (no relation of 'Gumley'), what was left of the previous hall then being pulled down. In 1865 it was purchased by George Allen Everitt, descended from a Norfolk yeoman family, and was inherited by his son, Major S.G. Everitt, and grandson, Horace, and sold again after the latter's death.

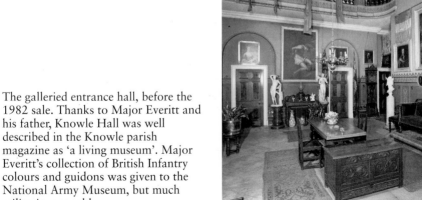

The galleried entrance hall, before the 1982 sale. Thanks to Major Everitt and his father, Knowle Hall was well described in the Knowle parish magazine as 'a living museum'. Major Everitt's collection of British Infantry colours and guidons was given to the National Army Museum, but much militaria was sold.

Sculpture at the 1982 sale. These Italian marble figures of the Four Seasons were subsequently seen outside an antique dealer's near Henley-in-Arden. Where are they now? South America? Japan? The plinths remain melancholy *in situ*.

The Royal Arms – often Hanoverian – figure in many of our churches, but this rare example commemorating King George V was formerly in the Knowle Hall chapel.

Major Sydney George Everitt (died 1932). Serving in the Royal Welch Fusiliers, he commanded the British Legation Guard in Peking after the taking of the Summer Palace by the 2nd Fusiliers Battalion. He was a magistrate, a governor of Solihull School (he wrote the school song), president of the Knowle Institute, Fentham trustee, and a governor of Lady Katherine Leveson's Hospital, Temple Balsall.

A group on the terrace at Knowle Hall, pre–1914. Major Sydney Everitt is to the right, his wife above; two sisters and a brother are also present.

Horace George Everitt, the third Everitt 'squire' of Knowle. He was a flight-lieutenant, president of the Knowle Royal British Legion, founder president of the Knowle Rotary Club, noted organist, chairman of the goverors of Arden School, and was also on Monyhull Group Hospital Management Committee. Horace Everitt died aged seventy-three in March 1982, and the sale of Knowle Hall followed.

Station Road, *c.* 1925. Years later, this became well known to the American servicemen stationed in the village, as their local headquarters and the 'American Huts', where they had their meals, were here, although they were billeted in private homes. Their generosity towards local children is well remembered.

What is now the United Reformed church in Station Road, built by John Wilson of Birmingham (1931–4), replaced the Congregational church of 1835 in High Street (sold again in 1994, becoming an Indian restaurant). It is described by Pevsner as if 'derived immediately from something German of 1922–3 . . . English critics will feel reminded of Ostberg, but Germany is much closer'. Miss Wootton calls it 'Dutch Colonial'.

James Carrico, from Kentucky, was one of a United States medical unit which arrived in Knowle in March 1944, remaining until August, before departing for France. Later he was to marry a Knowle girl – as did several other American servicemen. He and his wife settled in Knowle. His first billet was at Job's Close, which is now a home for the elderly.

Knowle formerly had its own cinema, built by Jack Chamberlain with his father's help. Did advertisements for 'Red Heels', and 'Lili Damita', in 1928, arouse comment in Knowle? Martin Harvey, in 'The Only Way', would have been innocuous enough! The picture-house, which had a small balcony – where the rain sometimes came in – was transformed into Johnson's Garage in 1955. Knowle, however, still has a fine village hall, and an operatic society whose fame is widespread.

Middlefield Hall (now demolished) was ceremonially opened in 1873 by the Earl and Countess of Derby as the Midland Counties Asylum, and described as 'a large and handsome brick building . . . built for about £6,000, with accommodation for around fifty inmates'. The more civilized name of Middlefield Hall was given when the National Health Service was introduced.

Workers at Grove Farm, Knowle, late 1950s, (left to right) Len Cotterrill, William Lloyd, Frank Brazier and Joe Bott are shown.

Section Two

DORRIDGE

In 1783 French immigrant Philip Frederick Muntz arrived in England, and is later described in Burke's Landed Gentry as of Selly Wick, Worcestershire. He married heiress Catherine Purden from Radford Semele, near Leamington, who gave him two sons and seven daughters; both sons became Birmingham Members of Parliament, the younger twice serving as mayor.

During the nineteenth century, the family acquired industrial wealth and country estates. Part of their Warwickshire lands were sold for a Paddington – Birmingham railway line, a condition of sale apparently being provision of a station, or halt, in what one ancient scribe termed 'Dorege'. Pundits translate this as 'wood, or clearing and ridge frequented by wild animals'; one adds that there were also human beings in scattered dwellings, such as Blewlake House, now sadly vanished. Opened in 1852, station begat village. If White's 1874 directory mentions a solitary shop – kept by grocer Mary Harris – others, and a gasworks would follow. There was already a hostelry just across from the station, a brick and tile works, asylum, and a horse-bus to Knowle. Well-heeled residents included John Marston, carriage-builder, at Parkfield, James Jones, draper, and James Booth, manufacturer; their businesses were all in the Birmingham. The hostelry, the Forest, 'Commercial and Posting', had been built by perspicacious George Frederick Muntz junior, old Philip's grandson, who later subscribed handsomely to a church. He laid out his land for 'villa-residences', and we can picture paterfamilias in increasing numbers returning to fresh air, with a welcoming family, cook and parlourmaid in attendance. 'Dorridge', says Miss Wootton, 'went on growing through the years', but it did not become a conventional district until 1940.

Growth after the Second World War would be tremendous. Clusters of smaller, if elegant, homes were to arise in place of single Victorian houses, though not all the older ones have gone; John Marston's Parkfield is flats. George Frederick would doubtless approve of such features as a covered shopping centre, the handsome Forest, still in Muntz hands, a public park, an exceptional village hall, and a wealth of trees; but Indian and Italian restaurants would surprise him. He could still take the train to London without changing. Despite fears of future development, Dorridge is a most agreeable place today. 'Wild animals' may be scarce, but there are great crested newts, foxes, herons, and the occasional kingfisher on the site of The Ards, a mansion now gone. One has even heard of a pet snake!

George Frederick Muntz senior (1794–1857) was a French immigrant's son. Uncompromising, aggressive (he once thumped a journalist who suggested he shaved off his beard, and was summoned for allegedly taking part in a church rates riot), he was a Liberal Member of Parliament for Birmingham from 1840 to his death. A member of the Political Union, stentorian in voice, popular with electors and in the Commons – where he is said to have been 'quiet'! – he made an immense fortune by the invention of 'Muntz Metal'. Republican, with an equivocal attitude to the abolition of slavery, in his last years he rented Umberslade Hall, presumably still exercising his noted gastronomic abilities. By Eliza Pryce, a clergyman's daughter, Muntz had eight sons and two daughters. A long and complex last will and testament left nothing to charity, and nothing to chance.

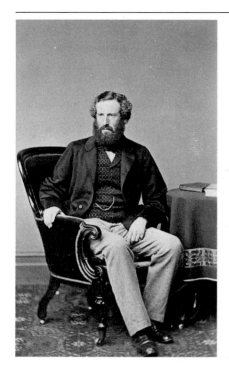

George Frederick Muntz junior (1822–98) heir to his father but a very different character (giving handsomely to good causes), moved from Beaudesert Park, Henley-in-Arden to Umberslade after his father died. In the Dorridge area he developed much land for 'villa-residences'. He introduced Scottish black cattle to Warwickshire. Sadly, he failed to enter Parliament. He built the fine Baptist church at Nuthurst.

George Frederick junior and his second wife, Sarah, daughter of Charles Aylett Keil of Aylesbury House, 1866. His first wife, Marianne, daughter of William Richardson of Calcutta, had given him two sons and six daughters. Only one son and one daughter married.

Built by George Frederick Muntz junior, the Forest Hotel was described in 1874 as the 'Forest Commercial and Posting-House', with billiard room, bowling green and pleasure gardens. Charles Lyons was the landlord. It is said that members of the Muntz family would spend the night there before catching an early train to London or Birmingham. Its most recent owner, Mis Yvonne Muntz, died in 1996.

The Forest Hotel on a frosty morning. No plaques, but guests since the Second World War have included John Betjeman (not then knighted) and Captain Knight with his famous eagle, 'Mr Ramshaw'; they were fulfilling local lecture engagements. The eagle was carried upside-down in its covered cage over the railway-line by one of the station staff.

The interment of a pet donkey belonging to William Edgar Muntz, which had hanged itself with the rope to which it was tethered. The burial party, left to right: ? Vines, Ted Whitehead, Sherl Chambers, ? Vines and David Goodey. The men were employed by Groves, the contractors. 'Willie' Muntz (1857–1930), landowner and second son of George Frederick junior, had a distinguished career as civil and military engineer in India and Burma. Extremely eccentric in later years, when living at The Dorridge, and taking his meals at the Forest Hotel, he alarmed people by his unkempt appearance, but one is told that he was really 'a very gentle person.' Others, however, say 'temperamental'. 'Willie' Muntz was the great uncle of Miss Yvonne Muntz, and she inherited the Forest Hotel from him.

Avenue Road, *c.* 1932. Many more houses have been built since this time. Woodland and tree-lined roads are still an impressive feature of Dorridge.

The Dorridge, or Dorridge House, 1892, when home to Mr and Mrs Charles Jacques. Earlier it was occupied by Dr Bell Fletcher, who had a small asylum, predecessor of what eventually became Middlefield Hall. Dorridge House has been demolished.

A group at Knowle and Dorridge station, *c.* 1914. Back row, left to right: H. Udale (goods carman), S. Wareing (porter), S. Britt (parcel carman), T. Atkins (Goods Guard), E.H. Margetts (junior porter). Front row: R. Barnett (shunter porter), B. Hoad (goods checker), C.F. Welch (station-master), C. Harris (booking clerk), W. Bennett (porter shunter), I. Russell (ganger). A freight goods engine is to the left.

Knowle and Dorridge station, *c.* 1928. Back row, left to right: Eric Wimblett, Arthur Farmer, Bill Moseley, Harry Udale, Harry Smith. Front row: Bill Daniells, Cliff Goodman (relief station-master), Jim Robins.

Knowle and Dorridge station, as it was then called, *c.* 1910, looking towards Solihull. Originally called Knowle, the name was changed in about 1900, eventually became Knowle again (causing no small confusion), and then Dorridge, as one hopes it will remain. Construction of the railway line, like the canal, must have had no small impact on the local communities.

Days of glory when the station had four tracks. It also had much better protection from the weather.

A grand procession complete with club banners, thought to represent rejoicing for a pre-1914 Coronation, but was it Edward VII's or George V's?

Another procession, apparently celebrating the Coronation of King George VI.

The Forest Hotel and Station Approach with waiting brougham, 1905. The buildings beyond continue the pleasing architecture of the hotel and are also part of the Muntz development of Dorridge. The well-remembered Dr Hollick had a surgery here.

Station Approach, c. 1935, when parking was easy. The road was originally Muntz property, but was sold owing to the nuisance of closing to traffic for Bank Holidays.

The foot of Station Approach, *c.* 1914.

The foot of Station Approach, between the wars.

Transformation scene: a new Midland Bank (below) replacing a profusion of daffodils. The site used to be a carpet of blooms in the spring.

The old Midland Bank, left, in 1951. It was superseded by the premises in Station Approach shown in the previous photograph, which back on to the railway. The shop on the right was Cock and Thextons.

Poplar Road with Aldington's shop about the beginning of the century. Frank Aldington, fruiterer and fishmonger, appears in Kelly's directory for 1908 and 1912.

Looking towards the old Vine Inn and the local gasworks in Station Road, 1951. The inn is now a private house; only the former gasworks office now remains.

STOCK SALE AT DORRIDGE

The stock sale ground, Station Road, 1927. Close scrutiny reveals that the farming community has since undergone some change in the style of dress!

A parish church from 1968, St Philip the Evangelist's served an urgent need as the Dorridge population grew. Thanks to the Revd R.W. Johnson of Packwood, land was secured and a small brick edifice built. It was designed by J.E. Payne and built for £1,000; principal subscribers were Mr and Mrs Philip Wykeham-Martin and G.F. Muntz junior.

Sadly, Philip Wykeham-Martin MP, who also gave the land, did not live to see the first public service in 1878, dying suddenly in the House of Commons library. He is commemorated by a window, and R.W. Johnson by a lectern. Large additions in stone, dedicated 1897, were designed by J.A. Chatwin.

A church procession from St Philip the Evangelist's, *c.* 1906, with appropriate banner and best hats. The Revd Spencer Aldridge, curate, left in 1905, and was succeeded the following year by Cyril St George Poole.

A group on the same day. The elegant dress of the girls is in striking contrast to the 'homely' attire of the boys.

Dr John Orton Hollick, sportsman, early motor-cyclist and motorist of Knowle, Packwood and later Rowington. A 'medic' of the old school, blunt, but popular, he was known to accept goods, such as furniture, in lieu of payment when patients were hard up. He practised from 1900 to 1926, together with other doctors.

John Woolman, who died in 1973, aged eighty-six, bought Broadacre, Dorridge (still in his family's possession), which had been the home of Sir James and Lady Curtis. He had an international reputation as a grower of chrysanthemums and other flowers. Broadacre was built early in the twentieth century, succeeding Marlpit Farm.

A peaceful scene of bygone days beside the Railway Inn on the road to Packwood and Hockley Heath. The inn has since been extended, but the front retains its old character. It is often called the 'Tavern'.

Aylesbury House, now a well-known hotel, is of varying dates. Property of the Aylesburys and their descendants for many years until 1917, it was frequently let, tenants including Mrs Helena Ferrers (from Baddesley Clinton), Charles Aylett Keil, father-in-law of G.F. Muntz junior, and J. Edward Payne, first architect of St Philip's, Dorridge.

Hockley Heath Institute was built in 1892 by George Frederick Muntz junior, but is no longer family property. In early days it was a favourite venue for large parties from Birmingham – two on the same day in 1895 numbered over 120 – who came in horse-drawn brakes. G.F. Muntz also opened a temperance coffee house and subsidized the Hockley Heath post office.

Umberslade Hall, near Hockley Heath, was built in about 1700 for Andrew Archer, and was rented by George Frederick Muntz senior in the early 1850s. Earlier, when it was a kind of nursing home, it was visited by Florence Nightingale, and the poet Tennyson was a patient. Bought by George Frederick junior, it remained the family home until the Second World War, when it was occupied by Czech, Belgian and other troops.

A convert to Baptist principles, George Frederick Muntz junior built a church for that denomination (eventually destroyed by fire) at Henley-in-Arden, and a much grander edifice with spire, clock and bells at Nuthurst, adjoining Hockley Heath, opened in 1877. Owing to ill health in later years, he had microphones installed and connected by wires to Umberslade Hall as he could no longer attend services; as Belton says, 'surely a foretaste of broadcasting!' The drawing is taken from Belton's *Nuthurst-cum-Hockley Heath* (1705–1848).

PACKWOOD TO TEMPLE BALSALL

After that brief glimpse of Umberslade and Nuthurst, let us make tracks for the quiet fields and woodland around Packwood and Baddesley Clinton, a shining pool at Darley Green, where the Fullards' waterwheel turned so long. (They had a windmill, as well, at what is now Packwood Tower.) Alas, Packwood's forge produces fine ironwork no more, but it can be found in homes not far away. There are old farmsteads, and moated houses. Ancient churches, too, one the scene of a wedding that was to have impressive literary consequences. Both churches are linked with a violent deed that led to abject penance, the crime contrasting with the life of Poor Clares in their convent and of a Victorian quartet evoking romance. We can hear of hunted recusants, or rejoice in lanes where hedgerows are bordered by the joy of 'Queen Anne's Lace'. The Fetherstons were prominent hereabouts for years, and Col. Charles Fetherston (d. 1831) lived 'in the style of an English gentleman also seems to feel a particular pride in being clad in the produce of his own estate. His hat, coat and underapparel, stockings and even his shoes are the produce of his own lands, herds, etc., and are manufactured and made within his own walls'. (West Warwickshire Directory, 1830).

It is very much the country of Edith Holden, the 'Edwardian Lady', who may be pictured gathering snowdrops at Packwood Hall, painting a waterlily at Packwood House, where sundials on Carolean walls greet visitors, and yew trees can be ghostly in moonlight. Kingswood has canal and railway history. Chadwick End and Bedlam's End confuse; which is which or are they the same? Chadwick Manor reminds one of climbing a baronial tower, a gardener's pride in hothouses with ripening bananas.

Past the delightful Dial House at Heronfield, and the site of cottages of forgotten silk weavers, Watery Lane leads towards Springfield. There are boyhood memories of walking along a traffic-free road, by lawns and cedars of a Georgian mansion designed by an architect better known for his work at Great Packington. The Blythe is here; this is 'Edwardian Lady' land again with a wealth of botanical interest. Temple Balsall astounds strangers, with a wonderful group of buildings. Thoughts turn to Knights Templar and Hospitaller, the benevolence of pious ladies, granddaughters of Robert Dudley, Earl of Leicester, and stone marries brick. A lovely, lofty church is close to dignified Temple House, old home of Blyths and Burmans and the Templars' Hall where massive tree-trunks, hewn in the thirteenth century, support the roof. Shawled and bonneted almswomen are recollected in Francis Smith's tranquil Court, clematis on gate-pillars.

Norton Grange, at Norton's Green on the road from Knowle to Packwood, sold by George F. Jackson in 1921. George Jackson was also the owner Springfield House.

Dormer windows went from Packwood Church at a Victorian restoration; then there were complaints that the nave was too dark! Nicholas Brome gave tower and bells as part penance for killing a priest (see also page 74). Dr Samuel Johnson's parents were married here in 1706. Moated Packwood Hall adjoining belonged to the Wykeham-Martins, but was long used as a farmhouse.

Packwood Church before restoration. Eccentric and lovable was R.W. Johnson, the parson at the time. He married the local schoolmistress, becoming so absorbed in the station bookstall on his honeymoon that train and bride went without him. He died in 1889 and no portrait of him seems to survive.

Members of the Haycock family of Chessetts Wood, haymaking, *c.* 1925. The picture includes, left to right: (1) Eric Wimlett (see Knowle and Station group), and (3) Harold Haycock, (6) Margery Jessie (Haycock), Eric's wife. Eric Wimlett took the photograph himself, using a cord attached to his rake.

The Haycocks on the haycart include Harold Haycock, far right. He supplied much family information, but unfortunately space does not permit complete listing.

The south front of Packwood House, c. 1756, before rendering obscured timber-framing. This old home of the Fetherstons, Elizabethan with Carolean additions, passed by inheritance in 1769 from Catherine Fetherston Leigh to the Dilkes, who then became Fetherstons. In 1869, however, with the family short of money, it was sold to George Oakes Arton, and in 1905 to industrialist Alfred James Ash, because 'the Boy', Ash's son, 'wanted it'.

The bee-boles in the terrace wall remain, but the bees are said to have been plagued by mice. The gazebo with pointed roof was subsequently demolished; a replica has been built. There is also a north-east gazebo (not shown) complete with fireplace and chimney to heat the adjoining wall for peaches.

Graham Baron Ash, 'the Boy', laid out a sunken garden between house and terrace; his Jacobean flower-beds adjoining fell victim to war and staff shortages.

Graham Baron Ash (born 1889), in court dress as High Sheriff of Warwickshire, from a portrait by William Dring R.A. 'The Boy' made the restoration and furnishing of Packwood House his life's work.

Educated at Radley, and serving in the Royal Flying Corps and Royal Air Force in the First World War (volunteering for the Second), he was known to his friends as 'Baron', which some people thought to be a title. James Lees-Milne described him as 'invariably spruce, dressed in well-ironed lounge suits which betrayed that he was not really a countryman . . . infinitely correct, yet not stiff or stuffy. Anxious yet welcoming. A trifle over-sensitive, yet infinitely kind'. One adds that he could be difficult, as anyone late for an appointment, or who rode on the outer courtyard grass, discovered!

Witty in conversation, 'Baron' loved entertaining in his immaculate house (no dog-baskets or tobacco-pouches lying about); the dazzling party he gave as High Sheriff in 1938 – Coldstream Guards band, gardens illuminated, marvellous food, footmen in powder – was to be long remembered. In 1941 he gave his home, many treasures, land and endowment, to the National Trust in his parents' memory, eventually retiring to Wingfield Castle on the Norfolk-Suffolk border. He died in 1980, having greatly contributed to the National Art-Collections Fund and the future of Norwich Cathedral.

Packwood House, 1868. The estate was sold the following year to George Oakes Arton. 'There was an unusually large attendance of Gentlemen present', says a newspaper account, 'and the most spirited competition was manifested for most of the lots. Packwood House, with its curious old yew tree gardens and home lands, realized £19,000'.

The famous Mount at Packwood House probably dates from the days of John Fetherston, who added the Carolean wing to his home; but most of the trees in the yew garden are mid-nineteenth century. The photograph was taken in 1868.

In August 1927 Queen Mary stayed at Castle Bromwich Hall with her friend, the Countess Dowager of Bradford. She toured several country-houses, including Packwood House, where she explored the yew garden, closely inspected a wealth of tapestries and other fine things indoors, took tea, and smoked a cigarette.

William Mumford in his coachman's uniform; he was Packford's oldest retainer at the time of Queen Mary's visit. The Queen stayed in her car until heavy rain ceased, her brother, Lord Cambridge, throwing a mackintosh to Mumford and telling him to put his hat on again!

Legends soon arise. Queen Mary did not stay overnight at Packwood, but departed after tea. The cloche hats are very different to Her Majesty's jewelled toque of shot-silver brocade. On her return to Castle Bromwich she received flowers from a garden at Catherine-de-Barnes.

The Great Hall, when Alfred Ash bought Packwood House, was described as 'a two-storey building of red brick, the lower part divided into two, with stalls for a number of cows and a harness room'. Queen Mary took tea here in 1927, only a temporary awning linking Great Hall and main house. The long gallery was added later. The 'fox' was only topiary.

The custom of erecting an heraldic hatchment outside a house on the owner's death, or that of one of his family, has almost died out, although many survive after removal to churches, where those in charge are mindful of our heritage. That for Graham Baron Ash, however, duly appeared, and is at Packwood House.

Station Road, Lapworth, as traversed by Mrs Dering (see page 75), who used the trains, if not cars, but disliked even the distant sound of them at Baddesley Clinton.

Lapworth (originally Kingswood) station, when a long-projected branch to Henley-in-Arden existed. Opened to passengers in 1894, the branch provided the first rail access to Henley, reached from Birmingham in three-quarters of an hour. It closed in 1917.

This bridge spans the Stratford Canal, near Lapworth station. Linked nearby with the Grand Union, the waterway is noted for barrel-vaulted lockside cottages, and runs from King's Norton to Stratford-on-Avon, ending close to the Royal Shakespeare Theatre. Authorized in 1793, financial problems led to long delay, and completion only in 1816. It figures in Temple Thurston's *The Flower of Gloster.*

The 'split' bridges are a feature of the Stratford Canal. The towrope for horse or donkeys was dropped through the central aperture as they passed round the bridge.

'It is this front which makes Baddesley unique', writes Roy McLeod, former Administrator. No other house in England exhibits so felicitous a blend of bridge, crenellated gatehouse and stonework of several periods, all on a relatively modest scale. A brick bridge, early eighteenth century, apparently superseded a drawbridge. This picture is taken from an old postcard.

The house encloses three sides of a courtyard; a fourth has vanished. The timbered work on the right was added in Victorian days, very successfully by local workmen. Baddesley schoolchildren used the punt when serenading the chatelaine, Mrs Dering, who sat at an open window – quite a Venetian scene! The picture is from an old postcard.

Marmion Ferrers, 1813–1884, depicted by his wife in the antique costume he affected. Descendant of the Norman Earls of Derby, and by right Baron Ferrers of Chartley, he was the son of Edward Ferrers and Lady Harriet Ferrers Townshend, and last Ferrers of Baddesley Clinton in direct male line. For some years, he and his wife shared Baddesley Clinton with her aunt and uncle by marriage. Mrs Ferrers eventually became

Rebecca Dulcibella (Orpen) first Mrs Marion Ferrers, then Mrs Heneage Dering, a self-portrait. She died in 1923, and is buried beside her two husbands and her aunt, Georgiana, Lady Chatterton, at the Poor Clares' monastery at Baddesley. A prolific artist, many of her paintings remain in her old home, others at the convent church and in Warwick.

Captain Edward Heneage Dering, 1827–1892, scion of an ancient family of Surrenden Dering in Kent, first married widowed Georgian, Lady Chatterton. Having actually asked for the hand of her niece and ward, Miss Rebecca Orpen, he was misunderstood by the elder lady, who took the proposal for herself, but he did afterwards marry Rebecca. Together with Lady Chatterton, as she continued to be known, he helped to save Baddesley from sale. He wrote novels of a strongly religious flavour, and was a considerable musician.

Georgiana, Lady Chatterton, widow of Sir William Chatterton, bart, in a portrait by her niece, after Brückner. Writer and poet, she knew the future Queen Victoria at Tunbridge Wells, and retained her old name and title after her marriage to Captain Dering.

Thomas Ferrers (d. 1970), in a (then unfinished) portrait by Kathleen Townsend. A great debt is owed to him. Distant cousin on the distaff side of the Ferrers family, he purchased Baddesley in 1940, assumed the old name, and, with his wife, carried out restoration, after bequeathing it to the National Trust. Unfortunately his endowment proved insufficient, but, after a gallant holding operation by his son, Thomas Weaving Ferrers-Walker, Baddesley was bought by the Government through the National Land Fund, given to the Trust, and endowed by two local ladies, Trust members and others providing funds for further restoration.

The lodge entrance at Baddesley Clinton, 1938. The gate incorporated wheels from a carriage belonging to a long-lived chatelaine (first Mrs Ferrers, later Mrs Dering), who did not greatly care for cars approaching her home, and only once, it is said, stepped into a taxi.

Baddesley Clinton Church and its surroundings are little changed since this early postcard. It is sometimes called 'The Church of the Expiation', a reference to Baddesley's lord, Nicholas Brome (d. 1517), who killed a parish priest whom he found 'chockinge his wife [Brome's] under ye Chinne'. As at Packwood, Nicholas built a tower, and gave bells in penance.

'Coo!' exclaimed a small boy, who evidently had never seen a moated house before, 'it's got water all round!' He might never have seen Baddesley Clinton, save perhaps as a 'Centre' for the sale of antiques, if it had not passed to the National Trust. A millionaire averse to visitors might have put a swimming-pool in the garden, displacing the traditional heraldic flower-beds.

That moat dates back to the distant de Clintons; much of the house seen in the early nineteenth-century drawing above is owed to the fifteenth-century Bromes, although the gatehouse has a grand Elizabethan window inserted by their descendant, Henry Ferrers, the 'Antiquary' and friend of the great Dugdale. It was Henry, too, who, despite poverty, even imprisonment for debt, inspired the wonderful array of armorial glass and carved chimneypieces in a house which would continue with his family in direct male line until almost at the close of the Victorian era.

The boy would hear the story of Nicholas Brome and the unwise priest, and would be excited by the recusant hiding-places that could defeat merciless pursuivants; and hear of visiting and unwelcome Cromwellian troops. He might not be as interested as his parents in the story so often told, of the Victorian quartet who between them were devoted to benevolence, music, writing of poetry and novels and prayers in a private chapel hung with old Spanish leather.

It is a magical house in a setting of unlandscaped park, trees, wild flowers, with a walk to the 'Church of the Expiation', where there is a carpet of bluebells in spring and the burial-place of Nicholas Brome, who died so penitently in 1517, requesting he lie inside the south door where people might tread upon him, as generations of his Ferrers descendants also lie there.

Staff and pupils at Baddesley Clinton School, before regrettable closure in 1990. Staff: K. Ritchie, B. Owyn, J. Mathews, E.J. Walsh.

Poor Clares (Collentines) from Bruges came to Baddesley Clinton in 1850; earlier there was a Franciscan academy here. The convent was badly damaged by fire at Christmas, 1983, but restored with the help of many donations, one from Buddhist nuns.

The old Tom Bedlam inn has been replaced and is no longer a hostelry. Chadwick End now has no village shop and only a sub-post office on certain days.

The Orange Tree, Chadwick End long before its late twentieth-century transformation. One recalls pausing there between the wars, Father ordering port wine for Mother and lemonade for me – which we drank outside! The name Bedlam's End and Chadwick End are confusing; the latter is now invariably used.

Chadwick Manor, a neo-Jacobean house, was built in about 1875 by Richard Ramsden. Later it was the home of Gilbert Wilkes who – lucky man – used to take long carriage drives in summer through the English countryside. Subsequently it belonged to the Watsons, was afterwards an hotel and is now divided into luxury apartments.

Dramatically set beside the Grand Union Canal, between Knowle and Chadwick End, the Canaletto Restaurant (the name since changed to the Bridgewater Hotel) was long the King's Arms inn, but familiarly known as the Cat in the Window.

Springfield House, in beautiful grounds beside the Blythe, was formerly Springfield Hall, Designed in the late eighteenth century for Richard Moland by Joseph Bonomi, it was afterwards successively the home of Boultbees, Edmondsons, Evesons and Jacksons, but is no longer a private residence.

George Jackson, JP, was a fine personality and hunting man (he was Master of the North Warwickshire Hunt), and a great benefactor to Knowle. He bought – and restored under W.H. Bidlake – the Guild House, a gesture unknown to the general public until after his death in 1948. The Jacksons left Springfield for Oare Manor, Somerset, in the Second World War, their Warwickshire home commandered as offices for Singers of Coventry.

Mrs George Jackson OBE, Red Cross Commandant. She and her husband converted newly built stables and garages at Springfield House into a hospital for convalescent servicemen in the First World War.

Charles Haycock, right, a member of the outdoor staff at Springfield House in the days of the Jacksons, and one of the Haycocks of Chessetts Wood. But who are the others?

A First World War family group, taken at Chessetts Wood. Left to right: Elsie, Charles (1881–1970), Ethel, Mary (wife), Doris Haycock.

The parents of Charles Haycock, Henry (d. 1928) and Matilda (Barlow), married 1876, photographed at Chessetts Wood.

Particulars of Sale

with PLAN of

THE DELIGHTFULLY-SITUATED VALUABLE

FREEHOLD RESIDENTIAL

and

AGRICULTURAL ESTATE

known as

"Springfield House"

KNOWLE, WARWICKSHIRE

WITH VACANT POSSESSION

OF THE EXPENSIVELY APPOINTED AND MODERNIZED

Georgian Residence

EXCEPTIONALLY FINE BLOCK OF GARAGES AND STABLING.

Two Excellent COTTAGES and Chauffeur's Quarters.

Well-timbered Grounds and Garden.   Fishing Rights in the River Blythe.

Together with the adjoining Capital

Agricultural Land

Park, Entrance Lodge, Cottage, Orcharding, Heated Glasshouses and Walled Garden.

Total Area, 196 acres, 2 roods, 28 perches

or thereabouts.

TO BE OFFERED FOR SALE BY AUCTION, BY

EDWARDS, SON & BIGWOOD & MATHEWS

in conjunction with

SAMUEL DAVY & SON

At the Grand Hotel, Colmore Row, Birmingham,

On **THURSDAY, MAY 30th, 1946**

at 2-30 p.m. precisely.

Subject to Conditions and prior Sale.

The Springfield House sale, 1946, when Springfield ceased to be a 'stately home' in the old sense.

"Speed the Plough."

NATIONAL FARMERS' UNION.

HAMPTON-IN-ARDEN, KNOWLE & SOLIHULL & COVENTRY

Agricultural

COMPETITIONS

HORSE & ROOT SHOW

WILL BE HELD AT

TEMPLE BALSALL, KNOWLE,

(By kind permission of Mr. T. T. Blyth),

ON SATURDAY, OCT. 3, 1925

£100 in Prizes.

CLASSES FOR ALL.

COMPETITIONS COMMENCE AT 10 A.M.

Prizes will be presented at 3-30 p.m., by

MRS. C. J. H. WHEATLEY

Supported by the President, Major C. J. H. Wheatley.

Admission by Catalogue, to be obtained at Entrance, 1s. each.

Entries close September 21st.

Schedules and Entry Forms from the Secretaries: *JAMES W. DAVY,*
J. R. BILLING,
S. WALKER,
Estate Office, Knowle, Nr. Birmingham.

An agricultural poster of 1925. Mrs Wheatley and her husband, Lt.-Col. Joshua Hirst Wheatley, lived for many years at Berkswell Hall, playing an important role in county life.

Lady Anne Holbourne, Robert Dudley Earl of Leicester's granddaughter, restored the ruinous church of the Knights Templar and Hospitaller at Temple Balsall, giving it a square tower. The nearby hall dates from the thirteenth to the fifteenth century.

Sir Gilbert Scott's extensive nineteenth-century restoration of the late thirteenth-century church included a tower based on the original, replacing Lady Anne's.

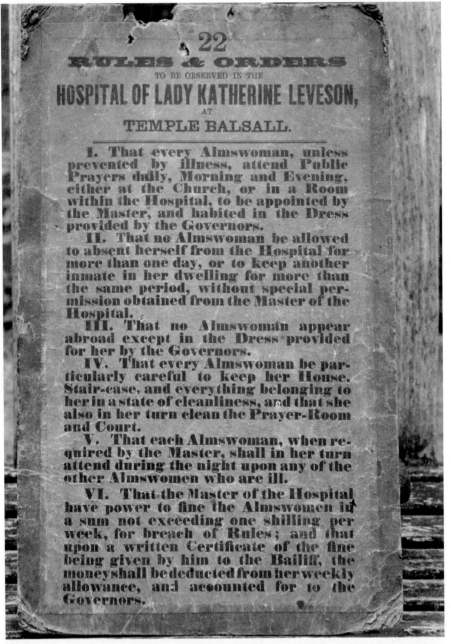

22
RULES & ORDERS
TO BE OBSERVED IN THE
HOSPITAL OF LADY KATHERINE LEVESON,
AT
TEMPLE BALSALL.

I. That every Almswoman, unless prevented by illness, attend Public Prayers daily, Morning and Evening, either at the Church, or in a Room within the Hospital, to be appointed by the Master, and habited in the Dress provided by the Governors.

II. That no Almswoman be allowed to absent herself from the Hospital for more than one day, or to keep another inmate in her dwelling for more than the same period, without special permission obtained from the Master of the Hospital.

III. That no Almswoman appear abroad except in the Dress provided for her by the Governors.

IV. That every Almswoman be particularly careful to keep her House, Stair-case, and everything belonging to her in a state of cleanliness, and that she also in her turn clean the Prayer-Room and Court.

V. That each Almswoman, when required by the Master, shall in her turn attend during the night upon any of the other Almswomen who are ill.

VI. That the Master of the Hospital have power to fine the Almswomen in a sum not exceeding one shilling per week, for breach of Rules; and that upon a written Certificate of the fine being given by him to the Bailiff, the money shall be deducted from her weekly allowance, and accounted for to the Governors.

Rules and regulations were strict at the Lady Katherine Leveson's Hospital, founded by Lady Anne's sister and established after her death in 1674. Prayers were said twice daily either in the church or Dames' Prayer Room. The 'hospital' is now called The Court of Lady Katherine Leveson.

The dress of the Dames at Temple Balsall included a shawl, grey for summer, red for winter. An example of the costume is preserved.

The bonnets and shawls of the Dames contrast with the costume of their visitors in this between-the-wars picture.

The picturesque bonnet and shawl are now only a memory. It is interesting to note that the Brethren of Leycester's Hospital, Warwick, founded by Lady Katherine Leveson's grandfather still have their gowns, silver badges and Tudor hats.

The green Court at Temple Balsall nowadays provides accommodation for men and women, in carefully modernized flats, with no bonnets or shawls, or stringent rules! The original buildings were by William Hurlbutt of Warwick, but, owing to poor construction, rebuilt by Francis Smith of that town, also responsible for the west wing of Stoneleigh Abbey. The Master's House beyond the lawns is a nineteenth century rebuilding.

The Rev. Robert Balleine with the Temple Balsall Choir. Mr Balleine was awarded the Military Cross in the First World War.

An anonymous newspaper correspondent (loaned cutting undated) wrote of 'the gentle and saintly Frank Fairburn', Master of Lady Katherine Leveson's Hospital and incumbent of Temple Balsall, and describes his beloved wife, Sophia, as 'a tiny little woman' who 'rose for prayer never later than 5.30 am, summer and winter'. Temple Balsall was one of the first places where Parish Communion and Breakfast began at the same time.

In addition to founding almshouses for aged women, Lady Katherine Leveson provided a school at Temple Balsall, originally for 'twenty poor boys'. The dress of the pupils in this pre-1914 group must surprise the children of today. The school has been rebuilt and extended, and is very popular.

There is frequent speculation about the name of the George-in-the-Tree at Balsall Common, but it has nothing to do with any Hanoverian monarch, as suggested. Under 1701, the Solihull Constable's accounts say: 'Expended at the George-in-the-Tree when I paid the High Constable 2/6.' Even George I had some years to wait before he came to England.

Section Four

KNOWLE TO HAMPTON-IN-ARDEN

The road from Knowle to Solihull crosses once lonely Copt Heath, near Longdon Hall, formerly owned by a poet's wife, her name preserved in Lady Byron Lane. It passes a renowned golf club and luxury homes – one with about the grandest gates in England! – dispelling any thought of bygone highwaymen. Diversion now excludes close acquaintance with Sandall's Bridge beside a Blythe widened for a landscaped park, but we see the 'secret' woods of vanished Berry Hall, and look down the lime avenue to more fortunate Malvern Hall. At Maid's Cross (not having taken the nearest way) traffic-lights mark our road to Hampton-in-Arden. There is a sight of Berry Hall woodland again; the mercifully surviving Old Hall, with its moat, precedes bylanes to Henwood Mill and Ravenshaw's rustic bridge, long a delight of artists. Catherine-de-Barnes proves to have been no lady, but named after St. Catherine's church there.

Over the motorway, noble trees herald the 'Tudor' mansion built by a Prime Minister's son, who became lord of the manor of Hampton-in-Arden and greatly changed the appearance of the village. (Mowbrays, who took the Arden name, were among medieval lords.) Legend says a lamp once burned on Hampton's church tower to guide strangers through wild country; certainly a landmark spire fell in a devastating storm, and was not rebuilt. The church has fine Norman work and a heart-shrine, and is neighboured by the Moat House with striking timbering. The High Street retains character, aided by Sir Frederick Peel's very pretty lodge and unusual pargetting. Hampton has enduring links with seventeenth-century George Fentham, the local boy who made good. There is fascinating railway history; Hampton station was once a junction, with a line to Whitacre, thence to Derby. A packhorse bridge and the sound of aeroplanes indicate other forms of transport, old and new.

The road out of Knowle village to Solihull on the Warwick Road is graced by delightful seventeenth-century cottages, seen here before restoration. The Knowle Society has planted thousands of daffodils just across the way.

Copt Heath, *c.* 1900. The once famous elms are traditionally said to have been planted by Robert Dudley, Earl of Leicester to commemorate one of Queen Elizabeth I's visits to Kenilworth Castle.

Longdon Hall, Copt Heath, replaces a moated manor-house of the Greswolds and Dabridgecourts, which stood on a different site. The present house, apparently incorporating some of the old timbers, was owned by Lady Byron, who established progressive schools in the neighbourhood. Godfrey Hirst was tenant in her day, the Clementsons being later occupants.

A quiet Edwardian day on the old road from Copt Heath to Solihull, near Sandall's Bridge. The building on the left was designed by John Soane as an additional entrance to the park of Malvern Hall, home of Knowle's joint lord of the manor, Henry Greswold(e) Lewis.

Malvern Hall, Solihull, before the removal of the central top storey and rebuilding of the wings after an 1896 sale to the Troman family. This was the chief residence of Henry Greswold(e) Lewis, who employed John Soane to enlarge the seat of his maternal forbears. Paintings and drawings of the house and surroundings by John Constable are now widely scattered: one painting is in the Victoria and Albert Museum, while another is in Cuba.

After an 1896 sale by a member of the Greswolde Williams family, Malvern Hall was reduced in size, but retained Soane's graceful porch and a fine staircase. Large additions, well sited, were made when it became a school between the wars. It is now St Martin's Independent School for Girls, and handsomely maintained.

Henry Greswold(e) Lewis (1754–1829) was painted several times by John Constable, who also provided a 'Mermaid' sketch for what became the Greswolde Arms. A portrait of Henry's ward, Mary Freer, is in New Haven, Connecticut, as well as a fine view of Malvern Hall.

Maid's Cross, Solihull (to revive an old name), before anyone thought of traffic lights. The thatched cottage disappeared in about 1895. The name probably commemorates an unfortunate maiden buried at the crossroads. In the latter half of the nineteenth century, my mother remembered the postman arriving on a bicycle and blowing a bugle. At this signal, people ran out with their letters for posting, there being no pillarbox!

Old Berry Hall, dating from the sixteenth century and long the home of the Warings, was partially demolished by Joseph Gillott, who restored the rest. The postcard dates from the early twentieth century. Outliving the 'new' hall, the house is still partly moated in wooded surroundings. There is said to be a 'friendly' ghost.

Joseph Gillott of penmaking fame built a new Berry Hall at Solihull in about 1870. Designed by J.A. Chatwin, it was noted for stained glass by Hardman of Birmingham and internal decoration by Lamb and Co., Manchester, as well as its arboretum of rare trees.

Taken in morning mist, the photograph shows the ruin of the 'new' Berry Hall. The site has since been cleared; the grounds, with walled garden and arboretum, are now a wilderness. The Solihull bypass bisects a former half-mile drive, and the fine entrance-gates (with the Gillott 'pen-nib' on the lock sold).

Ravenshaw Hall in the 1970s, a former Gillott property and seat of the Palmers. 'Good to look at', says Pevsner of this charming sixteenth-century house, which originally would have had a communal hall – the entrance-door to which would have been sited under the central gable.

Arthur Lewis of Catherine-de-Barnes with his baker's cart in Solihull High Street, 1923. Assistant Jack Smith is in the cab. Arthur covered a wide area in this cart. Dozing after a somewhat liquid lunch, he would be taken home quite safely by a knowing horse!

The name of Catherine-de-Barnes often puzzles people, not always strangers. It is derived from Ketelberne, medieval lord of Longdon. Often called Catney, or Catney Barnes, it was 'Kettle bern Heath' for Rector Clive of Solihull, 1840. It has a church, an inn, The Boat (rebuilt after a fire some years ago) and shops. There was a proposal for a railway line from Hampton-in-Arden to Redditch in 1842, with stations here, at Solihull and Salter Street. This came to nothing.

Henwood Mill, on the River Blythe, in Victorian days. It formed part of Joseph Gillott's estate when let to F.W. Hawkesford at £35 a year. The original watermill belonged to the Benedictine nunnery of Henwood, founded by Ketelberne. The mill has been badly vandalized.

In 1879 Joseph Gillott of Berry Hall built a school and church for Catherine-de-Barnes, sold as part of his large estate in 1904. The school is no more, but the picturesque building is St Catherine's Church and community centre. This picture dates from 1914.

Gee's shop, at the corner of Hampton Lane and Lugtrout Lane, Catherine-de-Barnes, 1920. 'The Place Names of Warwickshire' tells us in 1936 about Lugtrout Lane: 'As this does not lead from any stream along which a fisherman might have hauled his catch, the probability is that it took its name from some man called 'Lugtrout', the original holder of the name being perhaps a successful fisherman. The name appears from as early as 1609, so it does not refer to the nearby canal.'

Still going strong! The bakery, established in 1899, remains a family concern, and nowadays has branches in Dorridge and Coleshill.

A Victorian writer said Hampton-in-Arden was 'considered to be one of the healthiest' villages in the county, citing examples of longevity. It might not be today, if you stood in the middle of the road as in this early postcard.

A Victorian drawing of neo-Tudor Hampton Manor, built for Sir Frederick Peel MP. It was ascribed by Pevsner to W. Eden Nesfield, who did much work in Hampton-in-Arden, but by Tyack to a 'Mr Giles of Derby'; but a grand clock-tower was added by Nesfield.

Hampton-in-Arden's fine church dates back to Norman times, and has thirteenth- and fifteenth-century work, and a chancel carefully rebuilt with the old material last century. The west tower, vaguely seen through the trees, boasted a landmark of a spire, 'till', in Dugdale's words, 'by the extraordinary violence of Lightning and Thunder, hapning on St Andrew's day at night, in the year 1643, it was cloven and fell to the ground: at which time the whole fabrick, with the tower, were torn in diverse places'. Owing to parochial squabbles it was never rebuilt. The parish used to be far larger, including Knowle and Temple Balsall and a detached part at Nuthurst.

Hampton Church in the days of oil-lamps. Apart from such features as the sturdy Norman pillars, the church has the notable Te Deum Laudamus window, just visible over the altar, which includes Biblical figures, and portraits of writers and poets, including atheist Percy Bysshe Shelley, uncle to Sir Frederick Peel's first wife.

Hampton's Ring of Bells is no longer a hostelry, but the village still has the White Lion and The Engine (formerly Engine and Railway). This picture of about 1926 includes some interesting vehicles.

Sir Frederick Peel (1823–1906), MP and Chief Railway Commissioner, arranged for London trains to stop at Hampton station. A son of the Prime Minister, Sir Robert Peel, bart., he pulled down many of Hampton's ancient cottages; but with W. Eden Nesfield's help he provided attractive buildings in their place.

Unfortunately, Hampton-in-Arden has lost its pleasant Georgian vicarage, in favour of a – no doubt more convenient – modern house. It was the home of the Revd J.C. Adams, author of an outstandingly good history of the parish.

'The Young Music Makers', with the Revd J.C. Adams, 1940. He was Vicar of Hampton from 1939 until his death in 1957. An excellent musician and writer, his history of Hampton-in-Arden is outstanding.

Hampton High Street with inhabitants rather obviously posing for the photographer, *c.* 1900. Hampton Manor Lodge is in the distance, together with a glimpse of 'jettied' cottages with pargetting, unusual in this part of the country.

Nesfield's High Street lodge for Sir Frederick Peel's Hampton Manor 'tile-hung, varied and with white woodwork', receives praise from Pevsner, who describes the architect as 'a man of the dainty and intimate'.

Another reminder of Sir Frederick Peel's transformation of Hampton-in-Arden, with much help from the architect, W. Eden Nesfield.

A copy of a postcard produced by B. Reeves, Grocer, Provision and General Dealer of Hampton, though problematically the name over the door is C. Reeves. The village stores was run by a Mrs Martin from 1917–1953, so the photograph must have been taken before 1917, probably between 1912 and 1917, judging from other Reeves postcards.

A Hampton School group, 1897. On the left is Thomas Hope, master, who became a Grand Master of the Order of Oddfellows. Appointed in 1879, Thomas was head of the Fentham Endowed School for boys. The first schools under the Fentham Trustees were in private houses. A new school was built in 1782, and subsequently, additional premises were provided next to the original building. His son, Francis, is to the right in the front row. Descendants still live in the neighbourhood.

The Fentham Institute takes its name from seventeenth-century humbly- and locally-born George Fentham, 1630–1698, who became a wealthy mercer in Birmingham. A member of a local family, his benefactions are still enjoyed in Hampton and elsewhere.

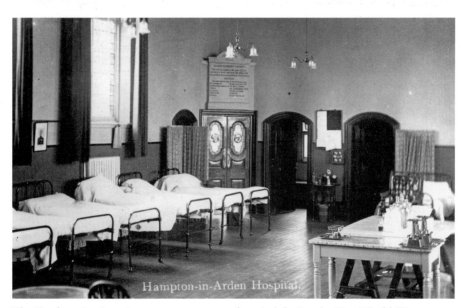

Hampton-in-Arden Hospital.

The Fentham Institute in use as a temporary hospital during the First World War.

Something of a problem picture, this is possibly a Women's Institute Drama Festival of the 1920s or '30s. Seated second right is Miss Ethel King of the Old Post Office; back row, far right, is Maggie Diggavy; far right, Alice Stingcomb; seated front left, Marsens or Mansens and Osborne.

Hampton station in LNWR days, 1906. It is not always realized that Hampton used to be a junction, with a line (closed to passengers in 1917) to Derby via Whitacre, but this declined swiftly in importance, and eventually was reduced to one train each way per day. Queen Victoria travelled this way when visiting Sir Robert Peel at Drayton Manor.

Not everyone is fond of Birmingham International Airport. This widely distributed poster was photographed in 1962 in Hampton.

Hampton-in-Arden, unlike neighbouring Barston, still has a post office – but not this one, which was still in operation between the wars. The postmaster, Walter King, who appears in directories before and after the First World War, was also a stationer, florist and parish clerk. I am told he also dug graves, and came to an unfortunate end when falling down the church stoke-hole.

A girls' school was built in the High Street owing to the increase in the local population. This was opened in 1849, closed in 1940 and the building no longer exists. An infants school had been amalgamated with this in 1906.

The Hampton-in-Arden cricket team in 1910. The clergyman is presumably the Rev. Charles Colthurst, Vicar of Hampton, 1908–1939. A 1912 directory also lists golf, tennis and hockey amongst Hampton's sporting activities. Visitors to the then very rural village were catered for by Mrs H. Cox and her Tea and Pleasure Gardens, three minutes from the station. She provided 'a large meadow and covered-in pavilion' for school treats and other large parties. Similar facilities were also at the White Lion inn.

Cyclists and motor-cyclists once gathered at weekends around the Stonebridge Hotel (and nearby Maltshovel) for drinks and 'shop' at the Holyhead–Chester road junction, now incredibly changed! The now-demolished hotel had a fine ballroom and other rooms in proportion, but started life as a simple country inn. This card was postmarked 1905.

Hampton's fifteenth-century packhorse bridge, 1907. This is a fortunate survival, as a nineteenth-century Vestry meeting wanted to demolish it. It was saved by the intervention of the Birmingham Archaeological Society.

BARSTON & EASTCOTE

Like Temple Balsall, Barston and Eastcote can hold surprise. One, perhaps, the number of 'gentry houses' – Eastcote Manor, moated Eastcote Hall, Barston Hall – scattered over an area near the treacherous Blythe, where, says the Victoria County History in an exuberant moment, 'the scenery is beautiful, but no woodland'. The approach from Solihull straggles delightfully through Eastcote to Barston village, which has thatch and seventeenth-century cottages. Alas, as too often, not so old directories reveal amenities gone: a glance at Kelly's in 1921 lists several shops, school, post office, Charlie George blacksmith, and coachbuilders (Findon, Pearson). The church and two inns remain, as at Knowle and there used to be splendid May Day festivities.

Manorially, historic names are prominent around Barston – Domesday Turchill of Warwick, Marmions of Tamworth Castle, Knights Templar and Hospitaller and Elizabeth I's Leicester again; Fishers, who rose in wealth and position via a Fisher, or Hawkins, who cried fish in Warwick Market Place. Dudley's widow was also lady of the Manor, 'excellent and pious' Lettice, Countess of Leicester, who, as you may read in St Mary's, Warwick, in what must be the longest memorial poem in any church, 'dyed upon Christmas Day in the Morning, 1643', but did great people ever see much of humble Barston? Perhaps Richard Hopkins, lord in 1694, prominent Whig in the 'Glorious Revolution', when James II was ousted, rode over from Coventry, where he, his son, Edward – Secretary of State for Ireland – and grandson, were all Members of Parliament.

Unfortunately, late Victorians could not let the early Georgian church alone, displacing most of the roundheaded windows for lancets; it is the 'Rigg Church' of a forgotten novel, *The Curate of Rigg*, by R.H. Hinder, Barston curate. Barston Hall and the Bull's Head (the Dragon) figure in a narrative reminiscent of Anthony Trollope – long out of print, but worthy of republishing, or a television feature! The story of a drowning in the Blythe is heart-rending.

Barston village, probably 1960s. It was the setting for a remarkable late Victorian novel, *The Curate of Rigg*, by W.H. Hinder, in the style of Anthony Trollope. Although the characters' names are fictitious, it must have aroused considerable comment at the time. Unfortunately it is now out of print.

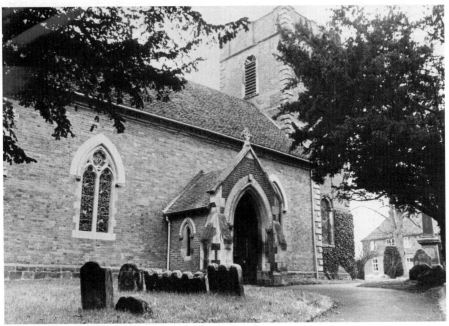

St Swithin's Church, Barston. Despite some Victorian meddling, 'Rigg Church' retains an early Georgian attractiveness, although a visiting bishop once called it 'the ugliest church in the diocese'! There is a fine open roof.

Georgian Barston Hall, *c.* 1900. It is described in *The Curate of Rigg* as 'a large solitary, square red brick house', simply 'the Hall', and the home of a manufacturer of flat-irons in 'Napleton' (Birmingham) – 'father of some twelve children, and as lively a set of young colts, mostly sons, as it would be difficult to match elsewhere'. This quite obviously is based on the Clive family, with their thirteen children. Dorothy Clive (Dolly) was born here in 1883, married a Clive (apparently no relation) and was the inspiration of a widely known memorial garden at Willoughbridge, near Market Drayton.

Barston has lost both its original post office, as well as the replacement, to the great inconvenience of local folk.

Mrs Mason, right, outside her thatched cottage, with her sister, Charlotte, early 1920s.

When this Barston School group was taken in 1911, nobody visualized the school's closure, the fate of many rural educational establishments. Barston still has its church and Bull's Head (the Dragon in *The Curate of Rigg*), with the Maltshovel not far away.

Eastcote Manor can deceive. 'An exquisitely pretty house, with its closely-placed timbers and decorative Tudor roses in the gables, two-thirds is actually Victorian, although it would be difficult to know that from a first view,' said *The Birmingham Post* when the house was on the market in 1995. (Early twentieth-century picture.)

The Riddings, Eastcote, one of the local 'gentry houses', was used as a hospital during and after the Second World War. The card is postmarked 1957.

WE ARE SURVIVORS

(For those born before 1945)

We were born before television, before penicillin, polio shots, frozen foods, Xerox, plastic, contact lenses, videos, frisbees and the Pill. We were before radar, credit cards, split atoms, laser beams and ballpoint pens; before dishwashers, tumble dryers, electric blankets, air conditioners, drip-dry clothes and before man walked on the moon.

We married first and then lived together. We thought fast food was what you ate in Lent, and 'Big Mac' was an oversize raincoat and 'crumpet' we had for tea. We existed before house husbands, computer dating, dual cars and a 'meaningful relationship' meant getting along and 'sheltered accommodation' was where you waited for the bus.

We were before Day Care Centres, Group Homes and disposable nappies. We had never heard of FM radio, tape decks, electric typewriters, artificial hearts, word processors and yoghurt. Only ladies wore earrings and a stud was something that fastened a collar to a shirt.

For us, 'Time Sharing' meant togetherness, a 'chip' was a piece of wood or a fried potato, 'hardware' meant nuts and bolts and software wasn't a word. Before 1945 'Made in Japan' mean junk, the term 'making out' referred to how you did in your exams.

In our day cigarette smoking tended to be fashionable, 'grass' was mown, 'coke' was kept in the coalhouse, a 'joint' was a piece of meat you ate on Sundays and 'pot' was something you cooked in.

'Rock music' was a fond mother's lullaby, 'Eldorado' was an ice cream, a 'gay person' was the life and soul of the party and nothing more, while 'aids' just meant beauty treatment or help for someone in trouble.

Those who were born before 1945 must be a hardy bunch when you think of the way in which the world has changed and the way we have had to adjust. No wonder we are so confused and there is the generation gap today!!

But by the grace of God we have Survived.

Acknowledgements and Bibliography

My grateful thanks for much assistance are due to: The Knowle Society (Mrs E.S. Warner, Mrs E.A. Stanley, Mrs V.E. Morton); Mrs S. Bates, Local History Librarian, and the Staff of Solihull Central Library; D.J.N. Green; T.W. Ferrers-Walker; Mrs P. Everitt; P. Davy; M. Bryant; Mrs B. Bryant; N. Roe; Mrs J. Roe; S.H. Bryson; Miss C.M. Adderley; A.A.P. Southall; D.R. Patterson; R. McLeod; D.E. Gibbs; J. Woolman; Mrs M. Sykes; H. Haycock; J. Carrico; Mrs J. Powrie; G.C. Burman; M. Fetherston-Dilke; the late Miss Y. Muntz; F.D. Muntz; B. Gallagher; E. Phillips; Miss M. Lines; Mrs E. Walsh; J. Griswold; Mrs B. Griswold; Mrs M. Binley; Rev. R. Watson Williams; Rev. P. Roe; Rev. J. de Wit; The National Trust (Severn Region); Warwickshire County Record Office; Birmingham Central Library; *The Birmingham Post*; *The Solihull News*; Monastery of Poor Clares, Baddesley Clinton; Curtis's Traditional Bakery; A.E. Lewis and Sons; Lionel Photography; John Wright Photography Ltd. My thanks also to all at Sutton Publishing who have made this book possible.

Every endeavour has been made to trace the copyright or owners of the pictures used within this book. In some cases however, this has proved impossible. Miss C.M. Adderley, 29 (bottom); Author, 13 (top and bottom), 36 (top and bottom), 74 (top and bottom), 83 (top and bottom), 98 (top), 101 (top and bottom), 111 (top), 115; Aylesbury House Hotel, 60 (bottom); Baddesley Clinton Archives, 76, 77; J.J. Belton, 62; *The Birmingham Post*, 84 (top); The Birmingham Post Studios, 81 (bottom); J. Carrico, 40; P. Davy, 11 (top and bottom), 12 (top and bottom), 16 (top), 18 (top), 20 (bottom), 24 (bottom), 31 (top and bottom), 42, 64, 87, 88; Mrs F.M. Dunn, 112; Mrs P. Everitt, 35 (top and bottom), 37, 38 (top and bottom), 57 (top); T.W. Ferrers-Walker, 17 (top), 47, 48 (top), 55 (top), 56 (top), 58 (top and bottom), 66 (top and bottom), 73 (top and bottom), 82 (top and bottom), 116 (bottom); M. Fetherston-Dilke, 67; D. Gray, 98 (top), 124; Knowle Society, 8(top), 10 (top and bottom), 20 (top), 25 (top and bottom), 26 (top and bottom), 27 (top and bottom), 28 (top), 34, 59 (top), 84 (bottom), 85 (top); A.E. Lewis & Sons, 102; Miss M. Lines, 97 (top); Mrs E.L. Lippiatt, 123; J. Marks, 113, 116 (top); F.D. Muntz, 45 (top and bottom); Olton Parish Church, 9 (bottom); Packwood House Archives, 68, 70, 71 (top and bottom), 72 (top and bottom); Packwood Parish Church, 65 (top and bottom); D.R. Patterson, 32; C. Reeves, 111; Mrs J. Roe, 42, 49 (bottom), 50 (top and bottom), 54 (top and bottom). 56 (top and bottom), 85 (bottom), 86 (top and bottom); E.C. Shepherd, 23 (bottom); Solihull Central Library, 8 (bottom), 9 (bottom), 14 (top and bottom), 15 (top and bottom), 16 (bottom), 17 (bottom), 18 (bottom), 19 (top and bottom), 21 (bottom), 22 (top and bottom), 24 (top), 29 (top), 33 (top and bottom), 39 (top), 41 (top and bottom), 46 (top and bottom), 48 (bottom), 51 (top and bottom), 52 (top and bottom), 53 (top and bottom), 55 (bottom), 56 (bottom), 96 (top and bottom), 97 (bottom), 100 (bottom), 103 (top and bottom), 104 (top and bottom), 105 (bottom), 106, 109 (top), 110 (top and bottom), 116 (top), 120 (top), 122 (bottom); Solihull Metropolitan Borough Council, 39 (bottom); *Solihull News*, 2, 28 (bottom), 30 (bottom), 120 (bottom); Temple Balsall Archives, 89 (top and bottom), 90, 91 (top and bottom), 92 (top and bottom), 93 (top and bottom), 94 (top); W. Thornton, 122 (top); Mrs M. Walsh, 81 (top); County Record Office, Warwick, 69 (top and bottom); L.N. White, 108 (top); J. Woolman, 59 (bottom).

Baddesley Clinton, H. Norris, 1897, London and Leamington Art and Book Co., Ltd.
Branch Lines of Warwickshire, Colin G. Maggs, 1994, Alan Sutton Publishing.
Hampton-in-Arden, J.C. Adams, 1951. Published privately by the author.
Our Griswold Family in England before 1693, B. and J. Griswold, Thayer Printing Co. Inc., Exeter, N.H.
Solihull and its Church, R. Pemberton, 1951, Exeter.
The History of Knowle, Eva Wootton ,1972, The Roundwood Press, Kineton.
The Stonebridge Railway, Roger Waring, 1994, Bruen Books.
The Story of Nuthurst-cum-Hockley Heath, J.J. Belton, 1948. Published privately by the author.
The Story of Packwood, J.J. Belton, 1951. Published privately by the author.
Warwickshire, (Buildings of England), N. Pevsner and A. Wedgwood, 1966, Penguin.

BRITAIN IN OLD PHOTOGRAPHS

Around Louth
The Lower Fal Estuary
Lowestoft
Luton
Lympne Airfield
Lytham St Annes
Maidenhead
Around Maidenhead
Around Malvern
Manchester
Manchester Road & Rail
Mansfield
Marlborough: A Second Selection
Marylebone & Paddington
Around Matlock
Melton Mowbray
Around Melksham
The Mendips
Merton & Morden
Middlesbrough
Midsomer Norton & Radstock
Around Mildenhall
Milton Keynes
Minehead
Monmouth & the River Wye
The Nadder Valley
Newark
Around Newark
Newbury
Newport, Isle of Wight
The Norfolk Broads
Norfolk at War
North Fylde
North Lambeth
North Walsham & District
Northallerton
Northampton
Around Norwich
Nottingham 1944–74
The Changing Face of Nottingham
Victorian Nottingham
Nottingham Yesterday & Today
Nuneaton
Around Oakham
Ormskirk & District
Otley & District
Oxford: The University
Oxford Yesterday & Today
Oxfordshire Railways: A Second
    Selection
Oxfordshire at School
Around Padstow
Pattingham & Wombourne
Penwith
Penzance & Newlyn
Around Pershore
Around Plymouth
Poole
Portsmouth

Poulton-le-Fylde
Preston
Prestwich
Pudsey
Radcliffe
RAF Chivenor
RAF Cosford
RAF Hawkinge
RAF Manston
RAF Manston: A Second Selection
RAF St Mawgan
RAF Tangmere
Ramsgate & Thanet Life
Reading
Reading: A Second Selection
Redditch & the Needle District
Redditch: A Second Selection
Richmond, Surrey
Rickmansworth
Around Ripley
The River Soar
Romney Marsh
Romney Marsh: A Second
    Selection
Rossendale
Around Rotherham
Rugby
Around Rugeley
Ruislip
Around Ryde
St Albans
St Andrews
Salford
Salisbury
Salisbury: A Second Selection
Salisbury: A Third Selection
Around Salisbury
Sandhurst & Crowthorne
Sandown & Shanklin
Sandwich
Scarborough
Scunthorpe
Seaton, Lyme Regis &
    Axminster
Around Seaton & Sidmouth
Sedgley & District
The Severn Vale
Sherwood Forest
Shrewsbury
Shrewsbury: A Second Selection
Shropshire Railways
Skegness
Around Skegness
Skipton & the Dales
Around Slough
Smethwick
Somerton & Langport
Southampton
Southend-on-Sea

Southport
Southwark
Southwell
Southwold to Aldeburgh
Stafford
Around Stafford
Staffordshire Railways
Around Staveley
Stepney
Stevenage
The History of Stilton Cheese
Stoke-on-Trent
Stoke Newington
Stonehouse to Painswick
Around Stony Stratford
Around Stony Stratford: A Second
    Selection
Stowmarket
Streatham
Stroud & the Five Valleys
Stroud & the Five Valleys: A
    Second Selection
Stroud's Golden Valley
The Stroudwater and Thames &
    Severn Canals
The Stroudwater and Thames &
    Severn Canals: A Second
    Selection
Suffolk at Work
Suffolk at Work: A Second
    Selection
The Heart of Suffolk
Sunderland
Sutton
Swansea
Swindon: A Third Selection
Swindon: A Fifth Selection
Around Tamworth
Taunton
Around Taunton
Teesdale
Teesdale: A Second Selection
Tenbury Wells
Around Tettenhall &
    Codshall
Tewkesbury & the Vale of
    Gloucester
Thame to Watlington
Around Thatcham
Around Thirsk
Thornbury to Berkeley
Tipton
Around Tonbridge
Trowbridge
Around Truro
TT Races
Tunbridge Wells
Tunbridge Wells: A Second
    Selection

Twickenham
Uley, Dursley & Cam
The Upper Fal
The Upper Tywi Valley
Uxbridge, Hillingdon & Cowley
The Vale of Belvoir
The Vale of Conway
Ventnor
Wakefield
Wallingford
Walsall
Waltham Abbey
Wandsworth at War
Wantage, Faringdon & the Vale
    Villages
Around Warwick
Weardale
Weardale: A Second Selection
Wednesbury
Wells
Welshpool
West Bromwich
West Wight
Weston-super-Mare
Around Weston-super-Mare
Weymouth & Portland
Around Wheatley
Around Whetstone
Whitchurch to Market
    Drayton
Around Whitstable
Wigton & the Solway Plain
Willesden
Around Wilton
Wimbledon
Around Windsor
Wingham, Addisham &
    Littlebourne
Wisbech
Witham & District
Witney
Around Witney
The Witney District
Wokingham
Around Woodbridge
Around Woodstock
Woolwich
Woolwich Royal Arsenal
Around Wootton Bassett,
    Cricklade & Purton
Worcester
Worcester in a Day
Around Worcester
Worcestershire at Work
Around Worthing
Wotton-under-Edge to Chipping
    Sodbury
Wymondham & Attleborough
The Yorkshire Wolds

To order any of these titles please telephone our distributor, Littlehampton Book Services on 01903 721596
For a catalogue of these and our other titles please ring Regina Schinner on 01453 731114